HOW A CITY WORKS

BY D. J. WARD · ILLUSTRATED BY VIOLET LEMAY

HARPER

An Im

Special thanks to Dr. Kelcie Ralph, Assistant Professor at Rutgers University, and to Kenyon Hunt P.E. for their valuable assistance.

The Let's-Read-and-Find-Out Science book series was originated by Dr. Franklyn M. Branley, Astronomer Emeritus and former Chairman of the American Museum of Natural History—Hayden Planetarium, and was formerly co-edited by him and Dr. Roma Gans, Professor Emeritus of Childhood Education, Teachers College, Columbia University. Text and illustrations for each of the books in the series are checked for accuracy by an expert in the relevant field. For more information about Let's-Read-and-Find-Out Science books, write to HarperCollins Children's Books, 195 Broadway, New York, NY 10007, or visit our website at www.letsreadandfindout.com.

Library of Congress Control Number: 2017959290
ISBN 978-0-06-247031-7 (trade bdg.) — ISBN 978-0-06-247030-0 (pbk.)

The artist used an ink brush, pastels, and scans of pretty patterned papers to create the digital illustrations for this book.
Typography by Erica De Chavez
18 19 20 21 22 SCP 10 9 8 7 6 5 4 3 2 1
❖ First Edition

*To Caeli, just because
she's wonderful*—D.J.W.

For Gray, who loves cities—V.L.

Some people live far away from cities. They don't live near other people. They might live on a farm or a cattle ranch. They might live in a cabin in the mountains. Or maybe on the shore of a faraway lake.

But most people do live in cities. Most people live with other people right next door.

Your city might have hundreds of people in it. Or there might be thousands or even millions of people living there. All those people need clean water to drink. All those people want electricity. All those people need safe and clean places to live.

And people need to go places. No one wants to be slowed down. And they need to be safe as they go.

How can you take care of all those people?
Your city has a plan for that.

Turn on the kitchen faucet.

splash!

Out comes cold, clean water. But where did that water come from?

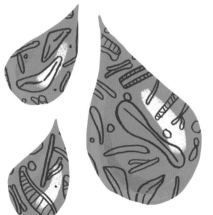

Most cities get their water from lakes or rivers. But water from lakes and rivers is not safe to drink. It has tiny living things in it called **microorganisms**. Some microorganisms can make people sick. The water may have oil or other harmful chemicals in it. It might have sand, twigs, or even dead fish in it too! All of that has to come out of the water before people can drink it safely.

Your city has a plan for that. Before any water goes to your house, it goes to a treatment **plant**.

   The treatment plant is kind of like an obstacle course, but for cleaning water. The water goes through all kinds of tanks, pipes, and filters.

Some parts of the plant remove dirt from the water.

Some take out harmful chemicals.

Before   After

Some get rid of the microorganisms.

Water might come into the plant cloudy and green and smelling like fish. But at the end, it's ready to drink!

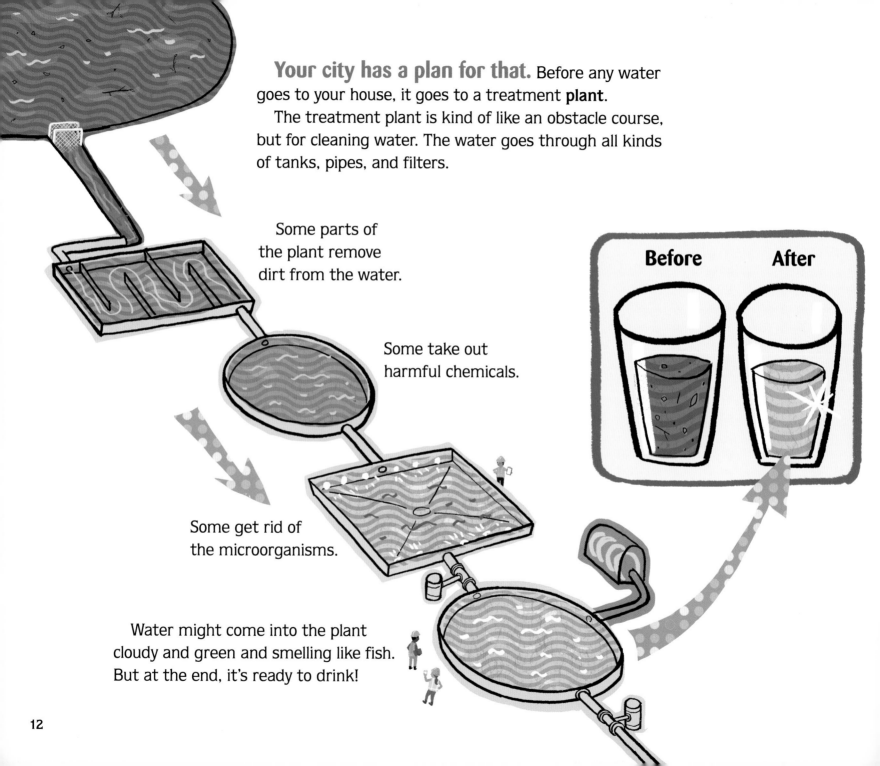

12

Once the water is clean, it can be sent to your kitchen faucet. Miles and miles of pipes carry the water from the treatment plant all the way to you. But where are they? They are underground! The pipes that bring you water are underneath the streets of your town.

splash!

That glass of water came a long way.

You have a light bulb in your room, don't you? Flick the switch.

Click!

The light comes on. Your next-door neighbor has a light bulb in her room too. So does the man down the street. So does your classroom at school and the gas station and the grocery store. All these light bulbs run on electricity.

GROCERY

THE GAS Mart

14

And not just light bulbs need electricity, of course. Refrigerators, computers, TVs, and microwave ovens all need electricity to work. Construction workers need electricity to power their tools. The hospital needs it to run machines that help keep people alive. All over town, day and night, people need electricity.

Somewhere in your town, or maybe in another town nearby, there is a big power plant. Inside the plant, they make electricity. Some cities use wind power to make electricity. Some use the power of sunlight. But most power plants make electricity using **turbines** and **generators** fueled by natural gas, oil, or coal.

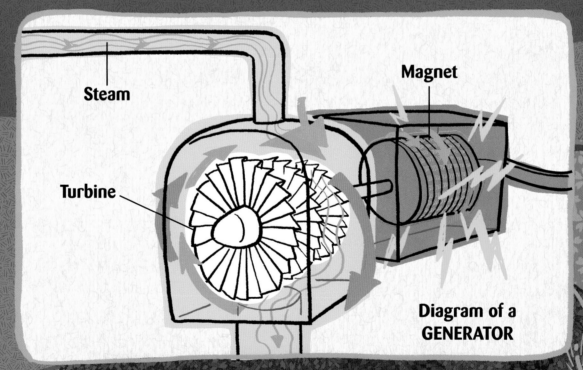

Steam

Turbine

Magnet

Diagram of a GENERATOR

Steam turns the turbine. The turbine turns a big magnet. The big magnet is surrounded by coils of wire. As the magnet turns, it makes electricity in the wires.

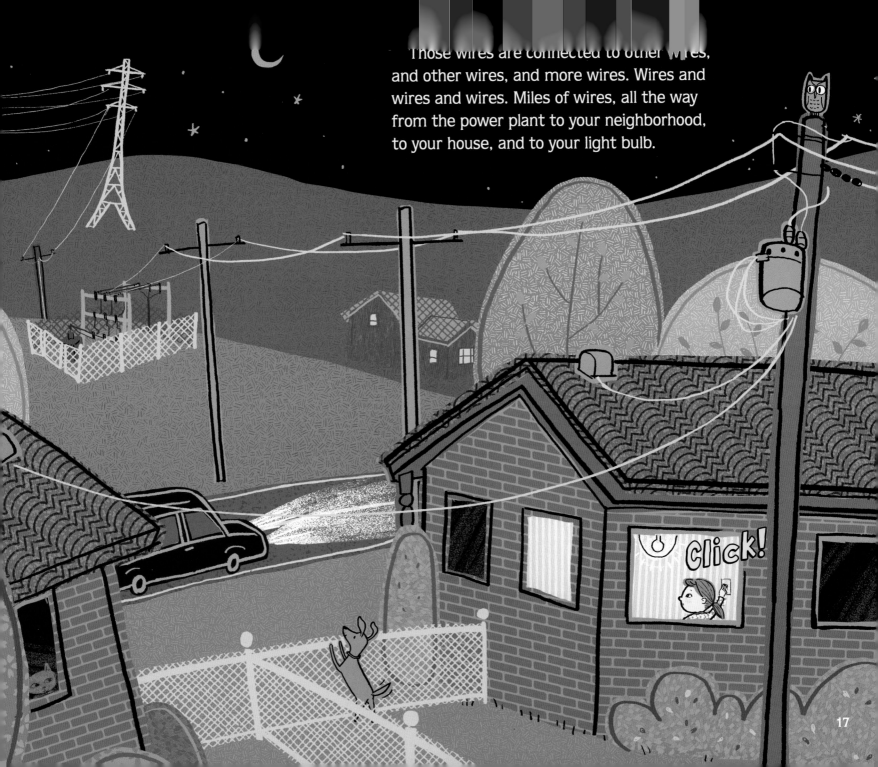

Those wires are connected to other wires, and other wires, and more wires. Wires and wires and wires. Miles of wires, all the way from the power plant to your neighborhood, to your house, and to your light bulb.

Click!

I have another question for you. I hope it's not too embarrassing. It's about toilets.

You have a toilet in your bathroom, don't you? When you flush, did you ever wonder where all the yucky water and stuff goes?

Your city has a special place for all that. It's called a **sewage** treatment plant.

Underground view of sewage pipes

Your toilet is connected to a pipe. Your sink, shower, and dishwasher drain into that pipe too. That pipe carries dirty water out of your house to a bigger pipe. The bigger pipe runs under your street. Your neighbors' dirty water goes to that same big pipe. Very big underground pipes carry all that stinky, gross, disgusting water and stuff to the sewage treatment plant.

At the plant, the dirty water goes into big tanks. Heavy stuff in the water (like sand, eggshells, and poop) sinks to the bottom, where it can be removed. Light stuff, like grease or oil, floats. It can be skimmed off the top.

That helps, but the water is not clean yet. Other yucky stuff, like pee and tiny bits of poop, is still mixed in there. Did you know that some microorganisms like to eat that stuff? It sounds gross, but it's true. So the plant puts them to work. The dirty water goes through a tank full of the good microorganisms. They eat the yucky stuff right out of the water! After that, the plant gets rid of any dangerous microorganisms in there. Now the water is ready. It can go back into rivers, lakes, or the ocean without harming wildlife!

Microorganisms

POWER STATION

GRIT REMOVAL

RAW SLUDGE

SLUDGE DISPOSAL

What was the last thing you threw away? A candy wrapper? An empty cereal box? Maybe a dirty tissue? Imagine if you couldn't throw it away. Imagine if you had to keep all your family's garbage! You might have to stuff it all into your room. Or maybe you would make piles of it in your yard. It wouldn't take long for your house and yard to be full of garbage.

All the people in your city are making trash every day. Imagine if all those people had nowhere to put it. Imagine if they just dumped their garbage in the street. Your city would become a big mess! Even worse, it would make people sick to have all that trash around.

So your city has a plan.

Trash trucks move around the city. They collect garbage from homes and hospitals, schools and stores, restaurants, office buildings, and gas stations. They collect it from all over town.

Some of the trash is still useful. It can be made into something else. Glass, cardboard, metal cans, and different kinds of plastics can be recycled. Special trucks pick up this kind of trash and take it to a recycling plant.

At the plant, the recyclable trash gets sorted. The glass, the cardboard, the metal, and the plastics go into separate piles. The different materials get bundled up and sent away to companies that can reuse them. The companies turn the recycled trash into new things! New bottles. New cans. New boxes. Even new carpet, car bumpers, and toothbrushes!

The garbage that can't be recycled goes to a different place. It's called a **sanitary landfill**.

A sanitary landfill is a place where trash can be safely buried. The landfill has clay or even a layer of plastic at the bottom. That keeps dirty water from seeping out. Each day, new trash comes to the landfill. Each day, a layer of soil is put over the new trash. Covering the trash with soil keeps it from spreading germs that could make people sick. It also keeps animals from getting into it.

Isn't that a much better plan than keeping all that trash in your room?

In the city, rain can be a problem. The ground is almost all covered by pavement. Water can soak into grass or dirt, but it can't soak into pavement. So when it rains, water just runs across the pavement. If too much rain comes at once, it can cause a flood. The water could flood into people's houses. But guess what? **Your city has a plan for stormwater.**

Streets in the city are not flat. They are higher in the middle than they are near the curbs. This makes stormwater run off the street toward the curbs. Curbs guide the water toward storm drains. Stormwater falls through the drains into large underground pipes.

Underground view of storm drains

The pipes carry stormwater to nearby streams. Once in the stream, the water can flow away from the city without causing a flood.

Some places in the city have no streams nearby. In places like that, stormwater pipes lead to areas where the ground is low. The low place might be a pond, or it might be a grassy park. Stormwater can soak those places without flooding people's houses.

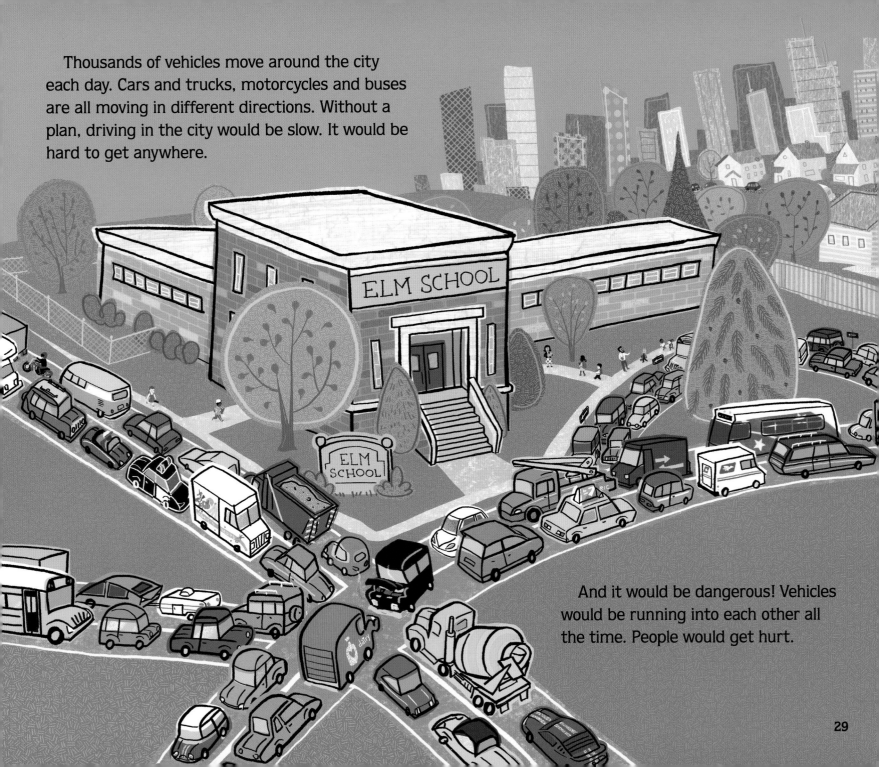

Thousands of vehicles move around the city each day. Cars and trucks, motorcycles and buses are all moving in different directions. Without a plan, driving in the city would be slow. It would be hard to get anywhere.

And it would be dangerous! Vehicles would be running into each other all the time. People would get hurt.

ELM SCHOOL

ELM SCHOOL

So your city has a plan.

Traffic lights and stop signs keep people from running into each other. Ramps make it easier for cars to get on and off highways. When trains come through town, bridges over railroad tracks keep the traffic moving. Bike lanes help keep people safe from traffic as they ride. Want to find a safe place to cross the road? Use a crosswalk or a walking bridge!

Buses, subways, and passenger trains help people get around the city without having to drive. When they don't drive, there are fewer cars on the road. That's less traffic! That's less pollution from cars, too.

A lot has to happen for a city to be a good place to live! And that takes a lot of people doing lots of different jobs. Some people clean the water. Other people make electricity. Some take care of the trash. Others design roads and bridges. And still other people keep everything running and fix things when they break. Without all those people working together, the city just can't run.

People working together.
That is how a city works best.

Find Out More

Cleaning Up Dirty Water

Materials:

- Water
- A clear mixing bowl
- Hot-chocolate mix
- Puffed rice cereal (or other cereal that floats)
- Raisins or chocolate chips
- A spoon
- Two coffee filters
- A funnel
- A clear glass

Part 1

1. Put clean water in the bowl, but don't fill it all the way. Leave some room at the top. That way it won't spill when you stir it later.
2. Put two scoops or spoonfuls of hot-chocolate mix into the water. Stir it up!
3. Pour in a cup of puffed rice cereal.
4. Add a half cup of raisins (or chocolate chips).
5. Stir everything up with the spoon so that it all mixes together.
6. Take a sip! How does it taste?

You have made pretend "dirty water"! When you stop mixing, the cereal will float to the top and the raisins (or chocolate chips) will sink to the bottom. In real dirty water, that happens too. Light stuff in the water will float, and heavy stuff will sink.

Part 2

1. Using the spoon, try to skim all the cereal off the top.

2. Next, try to scoop the raisins (or chocolate chips) off the bottom.

3. Now it's time to filter the water. Put the two coffee filters in the funnel.

4. With the skinny end of the funnel in the glass, pour water from the bowl into the funnel. Water will run out the bottom of the funnel into the glass. Pour slowly. Be careful not to pour too much! You don't want to make a mess. Don't pour all the water from the bowl into the glass. Leave some unfiltered water in the bowl.

5. Look at the water in the glass. That water went through the filters. Does it look the same as the water left in the bowl? It's not as cloudy, is it?

6. Look at the filters. Are they the same color they were before? They are brown now, aren't they? Where did the brown come from? It came from the hot-chocolate mix. It used to be mixed into the water, but the filters took it out.

7. Take a sip of the water in the glass. Does it taste the same as before? If you don't remember, take another taste of water that is still in the bowl. The water in the glass doesn't taste quite as chocolaty, does it?

That is similar to how water treatment plants work. Except water treatment plants are able to make the water perfectly clean. That way it can go back into lakes and rivers without making them dirty.

But sometimes it's good to have a little something mixed into the water, isn't it? Especially when it's chocolate!

35

GLOSSARY

Generator: A machine that makes electricity by turning a magnet inside coiled wire.

Microorganisms: Tiny living things that are too small to see without a microscope; some microorganisms can make people sick.

Plant: A place (often a large building) where something industrial happens (like making electricity or cleaning sewage).

Sanitary landfill—A place where garbage is safely buried.

Sewage: Dirty water that comes from toilets, sinks, and other drains in houses and buildings.

Stormwater: Water from rain or melting snow.

Turbine: A fan-like device that turns when it is pushed by wind or water. Turbines often are used to turn the magnets inside electric generators.

Websites to Visit to Learn More about How a City Works

Water treatment:
www.dcwater.com/kids/activities/
here_to_there/here_to_there.html

Electricity:
www.eia.gov/kids/energy.cfm?page=
electricity_science-basics

Trash disposal:
idahoptv.org/sciencetrek/topics/
garbage/facts.cfm

Civil engineering:
sciencewithkids.com/Science-Articles
/jobs-civil-engineers-do.html

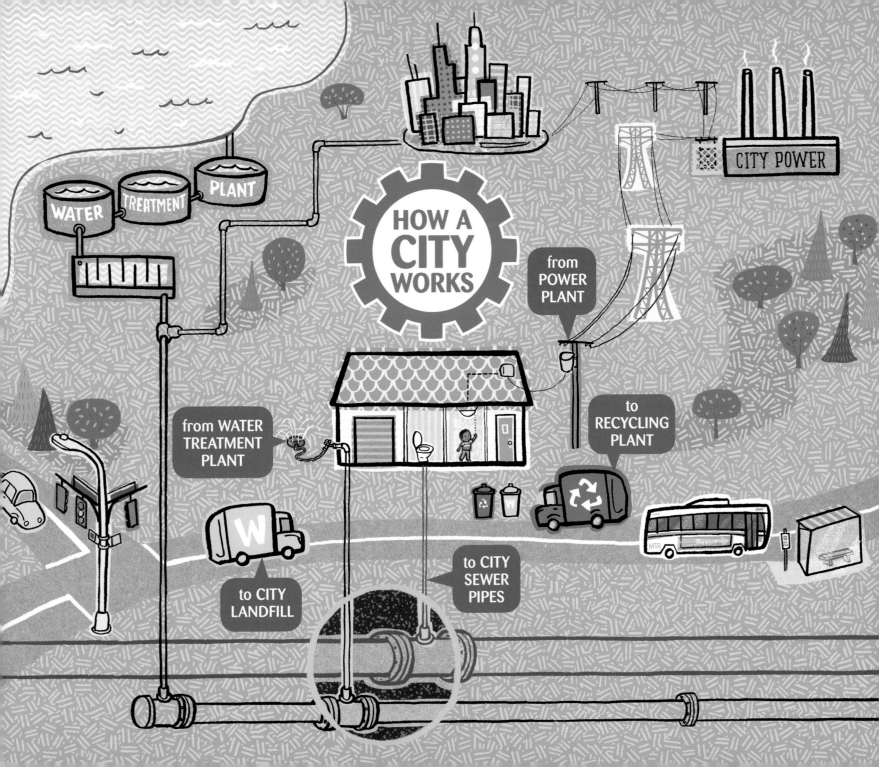

Be sure to look for all of these books in the Let's-Read-and-Find-Out Science series:

The Human Body:
How Many Teeth?
I'm Growing!
My Feet
My Five Senses
My Hands
Sleep Is for Everyone
What's for Lunch?

Plants and Animals:
Animals in Winter
Baby Whales Drink Milk
Big Tracks, Little Tracks
Bugs Are Insects
Dinosaurs Big and Small
Ducks Don't Get Wet
Fireflies in the Night
From Caterpillar to Butterfly
From Seed to Pumpkin
From Tadpole to Frog
How Animal Babies Stay Safe
How a Seed Grows
A Nest Full of Eggs
Starfish
A Tree Is a Plant
What Lives in a Shell?
What's Alive?
What's It Like to Be a Fish?
Where Are the Night Animals?
Where Do Chicks Come From?

The World Around Us:
Air Is All Around You
The Big Dipper
Clouds
Is There Life in Outer Space?
Pop!
Snow Is Falling
Sounds All Around
The Sun and the Moon
What Makes a Shadow?

The Human Body:
A Drop of Blood
Germs Make Me Sick!
Hear Your Heart
The Skeleton Inside You
What Happens to a Hamburger?
Why I Sneeze, Shiver, Hiccup, and Yawn
Your Skin and Mine

Plants and Animals:
Almost Gone
Ant Cities
Be a Friend to Trees
Chirping Crickets
Corn Is Maize
Dolphin Talk
Honey in a Hive
How Do Apples Grow?
How Do Birds Find Their Way?
Life in a Coral Reef
Look Out for Turtles!
Milk from Cow to Carton
An Octopus Is Amazing
Penguin Chick
Sharks Have Six Senses
Snakes Are Hunters
Spinning Spiders
Sponges Are Skeletons
What Color Is Camouflage?
Who Eats What?
Who Lives in an Alligator Hole?
Why Do Leaves Change Color?
Why Frogs Are Wet
Wiggling Worms at Work
Zipping, Zapping, Zooming Bats

Dinosaurs:
Did Dinosaurs Have Feathers?
Digging Up Dinosaurs
Dinosaur Bones
Dinosaur Tracks
Dinosaurs Are Different
Fossils Tell of Long Ago
My Visit to the Dinosaurs
Pinocchio Rex and Other Tyrannosaurs
What Happened to the Dinosaurs?
Where Did Dinosaurs Come From?

Space:
Floating in Space
The International Space Station
Mission to Mars
The Moon Seems to Change
The Planets in Our Solar System
The Sky Is Full of Stars
The Sun
What Makes Day and Night
What the Moon Is Like

Weather and the Seasons:
Down Comes the Rain
Droughts
Feel the Wind
Flash, Crash, Rumble, and Roll
Hurricane Watch
Sunshine Makes the Seasons
Tornado Alert
What Makes a Blizzard?
What Will the Weather Be?

Our Earth:
Archaeologists Dig for Clues
Earthquakes
Flood Warning
Follow the Water from Brook to Ocean
How Deep Is the Ocean?
How Mountains Are Made
In the Rainforest
Let's Go Rock Collecting
Oil Spill!
Volcanoes
What Happens to Our Trash?
What's So Bad About Gasoline?
Where Do Polar Bears Live?
Why Are the Ice Caps Melting?
You're Aboard Spaceship Earth

The World Around Us:
Day Light, Night Light
Energy Makes Things Happen
Forces Make Things Move
Gravity Is a Mystery
How People Learned to Fly
Light Is All Around Us
Phones Keep Us Connected
Running on Sunshine
Simple Machines
Switch On, Switch Off
What Is the World Made Of?
What Makes a Magnet?
Where Does the Garbage Go?

This book aligns with the Next Generation Science Standards.
Find out more at nextgenscience.org.

This book meets the Common Core State Standards for Science
and Technical Subjects. For Common Core resources for this title
and others, please visit www.readcommoncore.com.